Think For Your Self

With

INSPIRATIONAL WORDS

JOSEPH J.R. MATTERA

authorHOUSE®

AuthorHouse™
1663 Liberty Drive
Bloomington, IN 47403
www.authorhouse.com
Phone: 1 (800) 839-8640

Published by AuthorHouse   10/27/2015

ISBN: 978-1-5049-2932-5 (sc)
ISBN: 978-1-5049-5947-6 (e)

Contents

Introduction

"The next year is at the door." "Life is short so reach for more." "Laugh uncontrollably, and all the while never regret anything that makes you smile." Every day most of us hear and speak different words. Some words have lasting effects that linger in our minds. When I was young my home was filled with quotes and clichés. Many quotes seem to sound relevant to the times and never grow old, and some become old sayings over the generations. It is this love I have for quotes, song lyrics, and sayings that inspired me to compile the following work. This is also the first book of a series of motivational material that I intend to write in the near future.

After each quote there is an explanation or interpretation of what each quote means. Of course it is only this authors opinion. You may have your opinion and please feel free to write your thoughts below mine. Many quotes can be interpreted differently.

No matter what language you read or speak, it is the words that have a huge impact on what you think. Words are meaningful to everyone and mean different things to different people. It would be bizarre to live in a world with no written or spoken words.

In this book, there are quotes from famous people in history such as authors, sports figures, Presidents, and motivational speakers. I have some lyrics from different songs that I have heard through the years. There are quotes from people just like you and me, everyday people. I have also written a chapter of my own quotes, made especially for this book. One of these quotes however, was previously published in a column that I wrote in one of our local newspapers in south suburban Chicago Illinois from 2007 until 2009.

It is anticipated that this book will sit on the coffee tables next to the motivational readings, however what sets this book apart is its nature and format. I think of this book as the Rodney Dangerfield of motivational books. The G-rated version. I do hope it gets some respect.

You may find some quotes in this book that you have never read, as they were compiled in my spare time over the course of 5 years. Maybe you will find a new favorite or two. Sometimes just reading a quote may inspire you to have a great day. Maybe an inspirational quote will put a positive spin on your life and make it better. Very often it is the simple things in life that mean so much to us.

Motivational reading material is wonderful, but as we know at some point you must motivate yourself. This book is more designed to make you think. Read a quote, get inspired, and then maybe do something great. Remember it is you that must decide what you want to do with this wonderful gift of life. It is very difficult for anyone or thing to inspire someone. Although, maybe one of these quotes will be the trigger for you. People should try to help other people succeed whenever possible. It is very economical to pick up a book and learn for yourself.

When I was in college, I started reading the works of past philosophers. One famous quote from Socrates was, "First impressions are usually false," For whatever reason that quote sort of stayed with me. I often wondered after meeting someone for the first time if they were really the person that they portrayed. I suppose if you really think about what Socrates is saying maybe he meant we should not judge others by one impression. Or maybe we should not judge other people until they force us to do so. Perhaps if we all just viewed each other as brothers and sisters the world would be a beautiful place without much of the hatred and jealousy found in society.

Like most people, as I get older, I look at life differently than I did in the past. I suppose many people look at life differently as the world changes. People and things influence us in life, some good and some bad. The choices we make in life may decide our character and last a lifetime.

This book can go with you wherever your travels take you. You may place it on a table and read it whenever you feel the urge to try to inspire yourself. I tried to write it in a way that would be simple for everyone of all ages to read and understand. It is my hope that you will use these quotes and pass them on to others and spread some words of wisdom. It is wisdom that a man seeks his whole life and if it is found it should never be forgotten but only expanded upon and transferred to other people. It is my hope that this book as with many of the quotes enclosed will glide along through life and have meaning to you as they do to me.

The thing that I find most useful with most quotes is that they simply make you think.

The late great Earl Nightingale once said, "Men simply don't think." I hope that if nothing else, this book will help you. Mr. Nightingale also once had a quote which came right from the Holy Scriptures, "You become what you think about most of the time." If we really think, we can become whatever we want! Think and you shall become!

My late Grandmother had a natural instinct for spilling out one-liner's and she had some unique sayings. She was a real natural. I'm sure she never thought she'd be written about in a book. Many of her words are still with me today. Some of her quotes I will always remember.

I hope you enjoy my 100 favorite quotes.

This book is dedicated to my best friend who inspires me every day.

I am grateful to you forever.

Lovely Lola

Also to my wonderful Mother Marilyn who raised
me by herself and gave me the love

that I needed in life to become who I am today.

Motivational people

These are the people that try to inspire us to reach for the stars. They are the ones that make us look at ourselves and find out what we want out of our lives. The libraries and bookstores are filled with their self-help material.

Most of us want more out of life than what we have, and there is a certain "wonder" that we feel when a story is told about a successful person that achieves something great. If you are old enough, do you remember how you felt when Neil Armstrong first walked on the Moon? As a young boy I could only imagine what it was like to actually travel that far into space and then to get out of the spaceship and step onto the Moon. What was it that inspired man to invent a rocket ship that can travel that far into space? Who was the person that motivated someone to do this?

Motivational people can transform our lives if we only listen to them and do the things they say. What do you want in your life? Who inspires you? Perhaps one of the next 10 quotes will drive you into action and change your life forever. Everyone needs some motivation. Why not listen to the successful motivational people of the past and present and allow them to enter your mind, maybe you will get what you really want from your life. Who knows what can happen if you try to transform negative thoughts into positive ones and really try to be all that you can be?

Ask yourself these 5 questions:

1. What do I see myself doing in the next year?
2. What do I want in my life that is currently missing?
3. What are the places that I want to see?
4. What is it that keeps me from doing what I always wanted?
5. What makes me happy?

Maybe the answers will come from the 10 quotes of motivational people. Then after you are done reading this book try to come up with your own quotes and live your life as you want to, using your quote as your guide to find what you want in your life. Live in the moment and glide toward the future. Look toward the sky and wonder.

NUMBER 1

"Don't let the fear of time it will take to accomplish something stand in the way of your doing it. The time will pass anyway; we might as well put that passing time to the best possible use."

Earl Nightingale

Procrastination comes to mind with this first quote. How many times have we put off doing something simply because we are afraid of the outcome but yet not even know we are afraid? Many successful people fail and fail again before they get it right. Why not use our time to the best of our ability and try to accomplish what it is we set out to do. Everybody has the same amount of time in a day to use. Why is it that some people seem to accomplish so much while others seem to struggle all of their lives? Maybe it is because successful people seem to try different things until they find what it is they want and unsuccessful people don't bother to try at all? Or the disappointment may seem so great that the person feels overwhelmed by trying to change? Who knows? Perhaps a good doctor can help when things get too tough. One thing I do know is this quote really tells you to just do it. Follow your dream and have no fear. Fear is a terrible feeling and should not be part of your life. Become who you really want to become. Maybe this is the first step toward true happiness?

NUMBER 2

"What you get by achieving your goals is not as important as what you become by achieving your goals"

Zig Zigler

I was once told by a person much wiser than myself that it is not necessarily the goal or achieving the goal that is as important as the journey. The experience of accomplishing a goal is definitely a confidence builder and it can be exciting. I really love this quote because it has a simple message. The mystery is, you never really know what is going to happen unless you take action. The fact that you take the time to set a goal and accomplish it becomes a great human accomplishment which in many ways sets us apart from animals. The human mind is a magnificent thing that should be used to the best of one's ability. The life experience that you gain in accomplishing a goal is as important as accomplishing the goal. Zig Zigler says we should enjoy the ride along the way and get as much out of the experience or even more than the actual goal.

The old saying it's not how you drive but how you arrive. Achieving a goal is the result of hard work and dedication directed toward an achievement. The experience and the excitement of achieving something you set out to do can be a fantastic journey. The problems you face will build your character and make you appreciate hard work. When you achieve a goal that is important to you, it helps build your confidence and self esteem, which directly makes you an accomplished person.

NUMBER 3

"All successful people men and women are big dreamers, they imagine what their fortune could be, ideal in every respect, and then they work every day toward their distant vision, that goal or purpose."

Dr. Brian Tracy

Isn't this the summary of how the American dream can be achieved? To be successful is what almost all good parents want for their children. Schools are supposed to educate children and prepare them for the real world and most children believe early in life that they will be successful. They dream big and look at the world innocently. I think what sometimes happens to people is they lose sight of their dreams. They get caught in the everyday world of working and caring so much about others sometimes they forget how great they can be. If there is anything you really want and dream about, I feel you should give it the old college try because it is better to have tried and failed then to have never tried at all. There are many stories of men who became millionaires only to lose it all and become millionaires again. There are many stories about people who start second careers later in their life and become wildly successful. Remember the story of the late Colonel Harland Sanders?

NUMBER 4

"You have to put in many tiny efforts that nobody else sees or appreciates before you achieve anything worthwhile."

Dr. Brian Tracy

This quote seems to go along with the previous quote perhaps because it is the same man who wrote it. After you dream what you want and visualize it, you must then start the process of achieving it and this may take a lifetime, depending on the dream. After you accomplish what it is you set out to do, you may look back at all the little steps you took to accomplish your goal. For example let us say your dream is to build a "dream house". Think of all the planning and details needed to make it a reality. Finding land, buying the proper permits, having it surveyed, designing the structure, and this is before you even break ground. Think of all the details that go into the design. How important are those little details if one of them is wrong? Isn't it the little things in life that really mean a lot?

NUMBER 5

"When you change the way you look at things, the things you look at change."

Dr. Wayne W. Dyer

I heard this quote from an educational television program from Dr. Dyer. This particular quote meant a lot to me because after I started to think, it made me realize, there are always different ways to look at almost anything or any situation. What you may think is right may be wrong to someone else. If you are in a bad situation change the way you look at the situation and maybe you can figure a way to survive it or make it better. You can take almost any negative and turn it into a positive. I believe the world is made up by people and into this world or air, negative and positive thoughts are spoken and they almost equal out. You've probably walked into a room and felt some type of feeling either positive or negative, a phenomenon. What a powerful quote. Remember no one has the power to change you, except yourself.

NUMBER 6

"Fear is a little dark room where negatives are developed."

Unknown

Not sure when I heard this the first time but it sure motivates me to think positive or at least try to have positive thoughts. A friend of mine wrote a book called Mental Science 101 and in his book he states that many negative thoughts enter the mind on a daily basis. You have to train your mind into believing positive thoughts or it is quite possible for the negative thoughts to take over your mind. Perhaps this may be a basic explanation of how a person becomes depressed. Fear is certainly something most people are afraid of. Yet this very fear can take over a man's life and make him do things that he would never do. Find the fear, try to understand the fear, then conquer the fear, and you may set yourself free. We all want to be free of worries and fear. Once you have found out how to do this, think how much happier you can become.

NUMBER 7

"Think of your mind, your emotions, and your spirit as the ultimate garden. The way to ensure a bountiful, nourishing harvest is to plant seeds like love, courage, and appreciation instead of seeds like disappointment, anger, and fear."

Anthony Robbins

Tony Robbins is a modern day miracle worker for those that seek his services. He has helped many people change their lives. His ideas and words not only inspire, but they can turn you into the person that you always wanted to become if you let yourself. Your mind he says, is the ultimate garden. What do you plant in your garden? If you talk about love, courage, and being grateful and appreciative who you are and what you have done, then you have a world class garden and are someone that people will enjoy being with. Spread love in the world and teach your children if you are fortunate enough to have them, how to love others as you love them? Think how wonderful the world would be if we all lived with these thoughts.

Most of the terrible things that happen such as hate crimes and rape, happen because the people that commit these terrible crimes are full of fear and anger of someone or something in their life or past. If only those people would realize that the alternative is a much more peaceful way of life and if they could only change their way of thinking they would bring joy to others instead of hatred. Imagine what the late, great John Lennon said and sang. Imagine all the people living life in peace.

NUMBER 8

"It is in the moment of your decisions that your destiny is shaped."

Anthony Robbins

I like this because it is very profound. It almost sounds as if it came from the days of ancient history. King Arthur could have said this to one of his faithful followers. When you make a decision there will be some type of reaction or change that is directly affected by that decision. I believe in the end when our destiny is behind us, our decisions that we made, our choices in life, caused or influenced our destiny. It is imperative to make important decisions carefully. We should always think how our decisions will affect those people around us. Especially our families. If we are filled with love in our hearts then love will affect our decisions. Keep good thoughts in your head and good decisions will be made. From these good decisions a great destiny may transform.

NUMBER 9

"The world is full of people who are grabbing and self-seeking. So the rare individual who unselfishly tries to serve others has an enormous advantage."

Dale Carnegie

I first read this quote in his classic book, "How to Win Friends and Influence People." A book that at one time was required reading in many professional sales careers. Some people can be selfish and self-centered and some people are willing to lend a hand to a person in need. What type of person are you? Maybe it is the fast paced world we live in that causes people to focus primarily on their individual needs. It really takes a special person to care for other people. Special people help other people and that is really what makes the world great, especially when you meet people who are that way. When you encounter a person who is caring of others, try to honor that person because in today's society they seem to be rare. Become the person you want to be. Perform a self-analysis because as you know people can change if they really have that burning desire. My old Italian manager, from a job I worked at many years ago, used to have a button he wore that read, "you gotta wanna."

NUMBER 10

"One of the greatest gifts you can give to anyone is the gift of attention."

Jim Rohn

When you make a stranger feel good it makes you feel good. When you make a loved one feel good it also feels good. Paying attention to other people is such a wonderful trait to have. Instead of being all wrapped up in your own world, step outside of your self and make other people feel good about themselves. If we all felt this way and practiced this religiously we would all feel better about ourselves. Attention to detail can be a learned behavior.

Isn't attention all young children really want, along with candy? Children are innocent and young and they can be taught almost anything. My question is, what are we teaching our children in society today? Is it possible that we can reshape society by just paying attention to what the children are saying? Young children are usually paying attention to their parents. They may not listen the way we want but they are paying attention. They see what we do and try to emulate us. Be that solid role model for your children. The leaders of the family are the parents who pay attention to their children.

Notes

_____

_____

_____

_____

_____

_____

_____

_____

_____

The Spiritual Leaders

These are the people that are more in touch with their souls and spirits. They look deeper into the world and help us to find the answers to many questions about our existence. It is these Spiritual Leaders that try to influence us to find peace and love within ourselves. These quotes are moving emotionally and spiritually. They are the quotes that ask you look into your heart and find yourself.

Most of these quotes come from famous people, however there is one from a friend of mine who is a spiritual leader to me and to the people that know him. Whenever the need arises to be moved spiritually, I simply pick up the phone and give him a call. He has not failed me yet. At one time he was also my instructor. I think I even passed his class.

Take a look at these quotes and maybe one will fill your heart with something that will move you spiritually. There are certainties in life and one thing for certain is that we all need to be uplifted at some point in our lives. Think of the times when you may have lost a loved one or even a special pet. This was probably a time in your life when perhaps you looked for a reason or an answer. Spiritual Leaders can also be inspirational leaders and that is something we all need.

NUMBER 11

"There is no way to gratitude, gratitude is the way"

Mahatma Gandhi

The "great soul" Mahatma Gandhi tried to stop wars and promote peace during his lifetime. This particular quote is pertinent to me as a father. Being grateful for what you have rather than for what you do not have is so important. I have tried to instill this value in my children for many years. Gratitude must be the only attitude. We should all start our day with gratitude. Gratitude for the fact that you are awake. Gratitude for all the wonderful things in your life. Gratitude for experiences in your life, good or bad. Even if your life may not seem wonderful there is something you have in your life you can be grateful for. Change your life by being grateful for everything and every person you have ever met. If you start each day with thoughts of gratitude then your life will take a turn for the better and will continue to be wonderful. Do not skip a day without being grateful. Gratitude must be the only attitude.

NUMBER 12

"I have found that the greatest degree of inner tranquility comes from the development of love and compassion."

The Dali Lama

If you have love in your heart and peace in your soul how can you escape a feeling of tranquility? I love this quote because he is saying that if you can find love in everyone and everything, you will find peace. If everyone would lose their hatred and learn to love, just think what a better world this would be. There will probably always be crime and corruption in the world and nothing will ever be exactly right but we can only do our part. What part do you want to play? Would you rather spread love and peace or would you rather spread sorrow? Only you can make that decision. Find peace in your heart and you can help others find it as well. Inner tranquility is a wonderful feeling. Do you feel that serenity?

NUMBER 13

"You think that you are in this world, but I think the world is in me."

Hindu Master

How you perceive the world is your reality. As you look at the world through your eyes, the things you see, the thoughts in your head and your feelings, shape your reality. The Hindu Master says the world is in him. He has control over how he perceives his reality and does not let anyone dictate to him, unless he allows it, how he perceives his world. He may not react to the events around him until he has given it some deep thought. This is some deep philosophical thinking.

Every person has a reality. Each person's reality, as unique as it may be, brings a different perception to the world around them. Although people agree and disagree, there is a perception of reality that determines how one views their world. We all are kind of in our own little worlds and yet we all relate to each other on different levels of intelligence. As the old little man on the TV show from the sixties, "Laugh In," used to say, "very interesting."

NUMBER 14

"Familiarity breeds content and distance adds to enchantment."

Gopinathan (Gopi) Nair

This was given to me by a great friend and author Mr. Gopi Nair. This man is a true inspiration to me and to those who know him. I interpret this as meaning, the more you know someone the more you come to know their faults and weaknesses and this may lead to a feeling of content. If you have a friend that you have not seen for sometime you may think about that person with a feeling of enchantment. This distance or time gives one an opportunity to think about this person. Sometimes people we have known in the past just pop into our memories and this feeling may appear. In today's world, there are so many ways to communicate. The people you keep in touch with today may change tomorrow. Please do not take the people you love for granted as they will not always be alive for you to speak with.

NUMBER 15

"I believe that the purpose of life is to be happy. From the moment of birth every human being wants happiness and does not want suffering. Neither social conditioning, nor education, nor ideology, affect this. From the very core of our being, we simply desire contentment."

The Dalhi Lama

Show me a person that does not want to be happy and I will show you a miserable person. As we grow older we look for people, places, and things to make us happy. Sometimes it is the simplest of things that make us happy. The great Tibetan spiritual leader says it best when he says, "the purpose of life is to be happy."

Children are happy but yet many see their parents struggle or argue. This may cause the child to become unhappy. Then as they search for their own happiness, they change. Sometimes this may lead to drug use or crime. How many times have you heard an adult say that they just want to be happy? Happiness is probably the one common goal that everyone tries to accomplish. Many people think money will bring happiness. Others think a relationship will create happiness. Happiness is something that each person must find for themselves inside. Happiness is a shared desire. The greatest form of happiness is a state of bliss. Try to find bliss in your life.

NUMBER 16

"Our greatest glory consists not, in never failing, but in rising every time we fall."

Confucious

How true is this? I believe success is much sweeter when you look back and appreciate how hard the journey really was and the setbacks that occurred along the way to success. No matter what it is you want, you will not get it if you don't try or ask. A person must step out of their comfort zone. If you try something and fail, try again. Success stems from past failures. Very few people become successful without first failing. How many times did the great Thomas Edison fail? Many have failed and never experienced success. Possibly discouragement stops some people from succeeding after a failure. Pain and fear must be conquered in order to achieve positive results. Find your pain and discover your fears and then try to correct or alleviate them and maybe you will have taken the first step to the path of success. Success may be defined as discovering and fulfilling your dreams.

NUMBER 17

"Violence-free society, disease-free body, quiver-free breath, confusion-free mind, inhibition-free intellect, trauma-free memory, and sorrow-free soul is the birthright of every human being."

Ravi Shankar

This quote comes is from the spiritual leader not the late famous musician who played with former Beatle, George Harrison. This Ravi Shankar was born May 13, 1956. His first name evolved from a common Indian word which means sun. Coincidentally, he was born on a Sunday. Shankar has a goal for the world to become stress free and violence free. He has written various publications. Some of his teachings are related to breathing and relaxing the mind, using meditation. Even though Ravi is an author, I consider him a sort of modern day spiritual leader as it appears as though his goals and teachings are helpful in advising us how to live more relaxed and peaceful.

You do not hear the word birthright used very often in today's society when we are born we seem to be on display. We are taught most often by our parents in the beginning of life. Is it truly our birthright to be without violence, trauma, and sorrow? Then my question is why is this so prevalent in today's world? Violence begets violence and look at the world today. Racial violence in Baltimore and Ferguson. Murders are almost a daily occurrence in Chicago. We hear all about the terrible violence in the middle east that has caused sorrow throughout the rest of the world. My hope is some day the future parents whoever they may be can welcome their child into a peaceful world.

We should not talk about terrible events that are brought to us by the media almost every day. Rather we should discuss how to stop these terrible events from ever taking place. There must be solutions to our world problems and hopefully some very smart people in the future will discover these solutions.

Remember to spread love and peace wherever you go in life one person at a time and maybe together we can all change the world for future generations.

NUMBER 18

"Words have the power to both destroy and heal. When words are both true and kind they can change our world."
Gautama Buddah

This quote has a special meaning to me due to the fact that I have known some very sensitive people in my time and they are gravely affected by the spoken word. It always amazes me when a kind word is offered to someone how they light up. They smile and sometimes say kind things in return. Most people love to be spoken to with kind and sincere affectionate words. If everyone had a kind word for you and in turn you had a kind word for everyone you met each day, imagine how you would feel. As I wrote in the introduction it would be a bizarre world without the spoken word. Why not speak kind words to everyone you know. If you were angry before and said some things you wished you had not said, remember it is never too late to make amends or at least to try.

NUMBER 19

"An eye for eye ends up making the whole world blind."

Mahatma Gandhi

This goes back the word revenge and the negative force it provides. Gandhi promoted peace and stopped wars with his greatness and passive attitude. His hunger strikes are historic events that promoted peace. You cannot fight evil with evil as violence against violence only breeds more violence. It is possible that we may never see a day when the entire world is at peace. Try to find peace inside yourself and my hope is that you will spread it to someone else and all we can do is hope for a huge chain reaction. With all the wars and hatred happening in the year 2015 it is hard to find hope but that is what we must all do. Hope and love may lead to peace and happiness.

NUMBER 20

"Deal with the faults of others as gently as with your own."

Confucious

Take a look at yourself in the mirror. Do you see any faults or are you perfect in every way? Of course no human is perfect. It is easy to find fault with others but finding fault in your self and then taking steps to correct the fault is a much tougher challenge. We should all try to be gentle with others and try to understand, the real truth is, no one person is perfect in every way. If you have the ability to find fault with other people then try to use this ability to conquer your own faults and teach rather than criticize others. Remember to not find fault but find love. And remember once again that gratitude must be the only attitude.

Notes

_____

_____

_____

_____

_____

_____

_____

_____

_____

The Musicians

This is the chapter that I really enjoyed writing the most. The musicians are the poets, the spiritual leaders, the motivational people and they make the sounds that we love to hear. The classic rock and roll will never die. These were the sounds that filled my early years and are still filling up my rooms today.

As you will see these people wrote songs that were not only popular but had great messages. Unfortunately, you will only be able to read the words. I wish I could have included each song in the book and given you a set of head phones.

Songs inspire us and trigger our emotions. You may hear a song over and over and never get enough of it. There is nothing better than listening to a great old song that you haven't heard for many years. Sometimes these songs remind me of a moment in the past, a memory of great times gone by.

The great musicians have become almost legends and carry a certain mystique to me. These people lay it out there for all of us to hear and they expose their inner thoughts and feelings. Creative geniuses in their own way. If you are not a music lover then just read these simple words and move on.

If you are a music lover, specifically of these lyrics and artists then you may want to pull out the headphones and start relaxing to the sounds of yesteryear while you are reading.

NUMBER 21

"And in the end, the love you take is equal to the love you make."

The Beatles

This was the last line on the last album on their last recording as a band. The album was called Abbey Road, named after a street in London, England. The name of the song is, "The End." The Beatles were a band that sang love songs which inspired an entire generation of people. Primarily, John Lennon and Paul McCartney wrote songs with their wit and charm and in the end it was their music that lived on and has continued to prosper over 50 years later. George Harrison wrote some wonderful songs as well, especially in later Beatle years. Today there are many bands that try to emulate The Beatles.

I have always enjoyed their music, but more importantly I really appreciated the message they sent through music. In my opinion, Paul McCartney and John Lennon were two of the most creative songwriters of our generation. Unfortunately there are only two living Beatles, Paul McCartney and Ringo Starr. John Lennon was tragically shot and George Harrison died from cancer.

They sang about love and they put the music out there for us all to hear. The message was loud and clear. How can anyone not love The Beatles?

NUMBER 22

"I wish that I knew what I know now, when I was younger."

The Small Faces

Almost anyone over 40 can say this with sincerity. I always loved this song titled, "Oh, La, La." The Small Faces had limited success until they changed their name to The Faces, featuring Rod Stewart. An English rock and roll band who became part of the British invasion of music back in the 60's.

When I was a young boy, I always imagined that I was this older person and would fantasize about becoming a professional baseball player or a famous writer, but of course I had no idea what was needed to become one of those people until I got old enough to realize that I'd never play professional baseball, but maybe I could be a writer. Fame is not important to me anymore. If we only knew what we know now, when we were younger, what an interesting place this would be.

NUMBER 23

"There's nothing you know that can't be known, nothing you can see that isn't shown, nowhere you can be that isn't where you're meant to be, it's easy. All you need is love."

The Beatles

These are words of wisdom said like a philosopher. I always believed that most people can learn anything they want and within reason they can do anything they want. What stops us is ourselves. We put limits on ourselves in our own minds.

An old friend of mine said that he never had an original idea. He thought that everything he knew was recycled. What is true is we become a product of our past and the influences in our lives. The song was called, "All you need is Love." And as was usually the case with most of their songs the message was love. Lennon and McCartney came through once again with some profound songwriting.

"All you need is Love" was performed live on national Television in the late 60's. The Beatles appeared with flowers in their hair and there was love in the air that night in a world overshadowed by the war in Vietnam.

NUMBER 24

"Does anybody really know what time it is, does anybody really care, if so I can't imagine why, we all got time enough to die."

Chicago

What a great line from the band named after my home town. The song is called, "Does Anybody Really Know what Time it is?" The one thing we all share is time. Time in many ways is just a state of mind. I suppose when we are born the imaginary clock begins ticking until the end when we close our eyes for the last time. I once heard it said that time is just a state of mind. We make such a big issue of time because no-one has any time for anything. Give someone your time and you have given them the gift that they may have always wanted. This song tells me to try and live in the moment while we have the time.

Chicago was inducted into the Rock and Roll Hall of fame. They were an innovative band that intertwined jazz with rock and roll. Chicago created a unique sound and recorded many hit songs. They were first called Chicago Transit Authority but later shortened their name to Chicago. They still perform with a few of the original members.

NUMBER 25

"May your hands always be busy, may your feet always be swift, may you have a strong foundation, when the winds of changes shift, may your heart always be joyful, may your song always be sung, may you stay forever young."

Bob Dylan

This is the last verse from the song, "Forever Young." This is an inspirational verse and a very positive song. The song wishes the best to everyone. It seems the older we get, the younger we want to be. Some folks search for that fountain of youth, try to stay young at heart. I feel that Bob Dylan is a songwriter that really inspires you to think.

Bob Dylan once proclaimed that he compared himself to the troubadours of ancient times. In recent years, Dylan is still recording and touring at the ripe young age of over 70. Bob Dylan was inspired by folk singing legend Woody Guthrie. Bob Dylan, once named Robert Zimmerman, hitchhiked from Minnesota to New York City, where he visited Woody Guthrie on his hospital bed.

Dylan began as a solo act and became world famous for the songs that he wrote. Later in his career he became an electric group with a backup band known as, "The Band." Dylan was not always admired for his vocal ability, however his songwriting has no parallel.

NUMBER 26

"Take it easy, take it easy. Don't let the sound of your own wheels make you crazy."

The Eagles

This song titled, "Take it Easy" was certainly a classic back when I was a teenager. If you have thoughts that are not favorable and possibly depressing, these words, may possibly make you feel like you are normal once again. This is a good song for everyone. It makes me feel like sitting back and just taking life in stride.

This song has been recorded by many artists including Jackson Browne. It was stated in the Eagles documentary that Glen Frey and Jackson Browne both contributed to this song.

The Eagles in the early 70's, had a sound similar to Jackson Browne and Linda Rondstadt whom they collaborated with. Linda had that great female vocal range. Jackson Browne wrote some great songs and was a big success, even today. The Eagles had that beautiful harmonic sound. They were part of that Southern California sound of the 70's.

Recently, the Eagles have become more of a country sounding band. As with many of the bands of the 60's and 70's, they have done very little recording in recent times, however they did tour last year. This lyric is truly one of the all time classic lines.

NUMBER 27

"A well my hand is shaking and my knees are weak, I can't seem to stand on my own two feet, who do you thank when you have such luck?"

Elvis Presley

This line describes being in love or capturing that feeling like when we were teenagers and thinking we were in love. "I'm in love, I'm all shook up." As a young boy I experienced this weak feeling when trying to meet the prettiest girl in the neighborhood. This is such a great and simple song first recorded in the fifties. "All shook up," was a big hit for the late King of rock and roll.

Elvis Presley, born in Tupelo, Mississippi, had a real love for Gospel music. In many of his tours he would have backup Gospel singers accompany him. Elvis had arguably the most famous voice in music history. On the record, the song gives writing credit to an O. Blackwell as well as Elvis Presley.

NUMBER 28

"When you smile at me I will understand cause that is something everybody, everywhere does in the same language."

Crosby, Stills, and Nash

CSN first performed in public at Woodstock in 1969. They were introduced to each other by Mamma Cass Elliot from the band the Mammas and the Poppa's. They still perform live today, 2015. The song is called, "Wooden Ships."

This lyric kind of explains a universal form of communication, the smile. You can look at people and smile sometimes this will bring instant communication, a show of happiness or a connection. A smile is something that makes people feel good, as it spreads joy. We should all smile at each other, instead of frowning to see what a difference it would make. When you smile at someone you brighten up their day.

NUMBER 29

"Now that you've made yourself love me, do you think I can change it in a day? How can I place you above me? Am I lying to you when I say, that I believe in you."

Neil Young

Neil Young was born in Canada. He joined Crosby, Stills, and Nash and brought another dynamic to an already explosive sound. They wrote some famous protest songs including "Ohio" about the students that were killed by Police at Kent State College in the late 1960's. The students were protesting against the war in Vietnam.

The classic lyrics of two people breaking up, as the lines indicate conflict between two people. Trying to understand relationships can be a sensitive issue. The song is called, "I believe in you" from the After the Gold rush album in 1971. That particular record brought world popularity to Neil Young. He was a young man at the time and his lyrics, much like Bob Dylan really make you think. Neil Young has always seemed to be slightly different than most musicians of that era, truly a unique singer and songwriter. One of my all time favorites.

NUMBER 30

"How do turtles talk to one another, they just look, there's no reason to cover. Just like people they're drawn to each other. They don't live in no ivory tower"

Stephen Stills

The song is called, "Sugar Babe." It appeared on a solo album from Stephen Stills in the early 70's. The album included the hit single, "Marianne." Stephen Stills had a rock, folk and, blues sound. He wrote many interesting songs about life. Early in his career he played with Neil Young in a band that experienced some notoriety. The band was called Buffalo Springfield. Of course, Stills eventually became one quarter of Crosby, Stills, Nash and Young.

I always loved the analogy of comparing people to turtles. I find this humorous yet true. Some folks have a tenancy to crawl into their shell when they feel threatened. But it is true we are all drawn to each other, just like magnets or as Stills says just like turtles.

Notes

_____

_____

_____

_____

_____

_____

_____

_____

The Presidents

These were the leaders of our country. Many of their words commanded respect and honor. They were elected by us, the people of the United States of America. Some of the past quotes from these great men still ring true today. When I was in school it was important to know who the past presidents were and the order that they became elected.

George Washington was called the Father of Our Country. He was the first president elected. He had the famous story of the cherry tree, how he could not tell a lie. How many politicians and presidents still honor this belief? Imagine if all politicians never told a lie or were never corrupt.

Another famous president was Abraham Lincoln. He was the sixteenth president of our great country and he was remembered for being instrumental in the freeing of slavery in America. Lincoln was assassinated in 1865.

Many quotes from our past presidents spoke words that later in life they may have regretted. Remember George Bush, "read my lips?" Even with that quote as we know his son became president and recently, his other son announced that he will run for the Republican nomination for president in 2016.

Ronald Regan was a famous president from Illinois. Who was your favorite president? Do you have a memorable quote from one of our past leaders?

NUMBER 31

"Tis better to be silent and be thought a fool, than to speak and remove all doubt."

Abraham Lincoln

This was actually a favorite quote of my daughter's but I picked it up and when I read it, it really rang true and we laughed together. How many of us in our lives have said things to someone without really thinking it through. I know I have done it many times in the past, but as I get older I realize how important it is to think about what you are going to say before you actually utter the words.

NUMBER 32

"We should not let our fears hold us back from pursuing our hopes"

John Fitzgerald Kennedy

I believe everyone is afraid of someone or something. Fear is a feeling that if we are able to overcome can bring tremendous results. If we as a country have any hope at all, we must not be afraid to believe good things are possible. Kennedy said, "we must pursue our hopes," and I like to add, "our dreams," to that phrase. Hopes and dreams are the foundation of this great nation.

NUMBER 33

"Let me assert my firm belief that the only thing to fear is fear itself."

Franklin D. Roosevelt

Staying on the topic of fear seems topical these days with the threat of terrorism almost happening daily. When our country was attacked on September 11th 2001, our great country changed tremendously. There seems to be more cynicism in the air as I believe people our trying to mask their fear. There are many things people are afraid of today, probably more than ever before in the history of our world. Many of these fears are elaborated on by our media. This quote was meaningful in Roosevelt's day and still remains true today. We should try to overcome fear to accomplish great things in life. To be afraid, brings uncertainty. Uncertainty brings the unknown and with the unknown, fear may follow.

NUMBER 34

"History does not long entrust the care of freedom to the weak or the timid."

Dwight D. Eisenhower

The freedom that made our country the land of the free and the home of the brave over 200 years ago should never be forgotten. This is our country's history. The people who fought to create a place where anyone can come and make a life for themselves and their families were not weak or timid people. These people were some of the bravest people to ever live. Freedom comes at a large cost. Many lives were sacrificed in the many wars that were fought throughout history in order to let me have the freedom to write this so that you can read it today.

NUMBER 35

"Our constitution works. Our great republic is a government of laws, not of men."

Gerald Ford

Again our country started with great leaders who created the constitution which still performs its job, over 200 years later. The government is supposed to be above men unfortunately some people try to put themselves above the government. The law is supposed to bring order and control to the insane things that some people do, such as commit murder. As the world changes sometimes changes in our constitution may be necessary, however, these changes will dictate the future of our children's lives. Great thought and discussion should be put into any changes in our nation.

NUMBER 36

"We need a new spirit of community, a sense that we are all in this together, or the American Dream will continue to wither. Our destiny is bound up with the destiny of every other American."

Bill Clinton

No one person is all alone, even if the person lives alone on an island and is a recluse. We all live in this world together and to raise our spirit to high limits. If we think and believe in positive thinking, it will help to eliminate the fear that overlooks our country today. This country was built on dreams of freedom and the American dream can be whatever anyone wants in life. We all need to believe in ourselves and our country. It is also important to help the less fortunate souls in our world.

NUMBER 37

"A strong nation, like a strong person, can afford to be gentle, firm, thoughtful, and restrained. It can afford to extend a helping hand to others. It's a weak nation, like a weak person, that must behave with bluster and boasting and rashness and other signs of insecurity."

Jimmy Carter

Powerful, strong, and brave are words that have always been associated with our great country. In recent years, some of our weaknesses have been revealed but overall we are still a strong nation. I believe it was always our thoughtfulness as a nation that made our country great. Other countries could always depend on us when they were in dire straits. Things have changed since the war in Iraq. Perhaps some insecurity has been revealed. We must still believe in our country as a great nation. When this war is over and our brave people come home, our country can begin to rebuild itself into the strong, firm, thoughtful nation that we are.

NUMBER 38

"I hope I shall always possess firmness and virtue enough to maintain what I consider the most enviable of all titles, the character of an Honest Man."

George Washington

The first President, the father of our country George Washington had many famous quotes; this was always one of my favorites. Think for moment if all politicians believed and lived by this quote. If we all felt that our government was completely honest with us what a different world we would live in today. Leadership starts at the top and perhaps the reason that most people, with good reason, are untrusting is because of the examples set by our politicians. Leadership starts at the top and trickles down to the people.

NUMBER 39

"Determine never to be idle. No person will have occasion to complain of the want of time who never loses any. It is wonderful how much may be done if we are always doing."

Thomas Jefferson

This was obviously written before television and video games. People can accomplish so much in life just by not being idle. Imagine what Thomas Jefferson could have accomplished in this day and age with the information that is available today at our fingertips. Keep on working toward your dreams and goals and never stop thinking about what you want or who you want to become, because as far as we know we only get one shot at this wonderful thing called life.

NUMBER 40

"Each generation goes further than the generation preceding it because it stands on the shoulders of that generation. You will have opportunities beyond anything we've ever known."

Ronald Reagan

It seems to be true that each generation gets a little smarter. Maybe because the human mind is still evolving or could it be the next generation learns from the previous generation and can hopefully improves on their mistakes. Either way the opportunities are certainly endless and President Reagan was a president that had many great quotes. I like this quote because it provides a positive spin on the future of the country. We need to read quotes like this in order to feel good about the future of our country.

Notes

_____

_____

_____

_____

_____

_____

_____

_____

The Athletes

The famous athletes of our times are important because they are performing at the top of their profession. They are hero's to young and old. They play games we loved as children and adults and because of this, their words seem important to us. Today there is major coverage from the media on a daily basis. ESPN brought worldwide sports coverage to our country in the early 80's. This is one reason that I have included quotes from famous athletes.

Another reason I included quotes of famous athletes is because of my love of sports. As a youngster, I played and enjoyed baseball in the summer and hockey in the winter. I also played some basketball and football. Like every one of my friends we had our favorite players who we tried to emulate. The way I swing a baseball bat was influenced by a famous baseball player. The reason I shot left-handed with a hockey stick was because of the great Bobby Hull. The voice of Mr. Petit on the radio, late at night, "A shot and a goal."

Sports bring out the competitive nature in people. It has excitement and caries interest as seasons unfold. Each year is special. The spring always reminds me of the start of the baseball season. The spring is also when the playoffs start in hockey and basketball. Winter is associated with football. The super bowl in late January or early February has become somewhat of an American event, maybe someday it will be an American holiday.

I hope you enjoy the quotes from some famous athletes.

NUMBER 41

"You must try to generate happiness within yourself. If you aren't happy in one place, chances are you won't be happy anyplace."

Ernie Banks

Ernie Banks was a unique man when he started his career in Chicago; he was a black baseball player, who played when segregation stained our country. Ernie was somewhat of a pioneer in Chicago baseball history. At the time, he broke into the major leagues great black baseball players were just beginning to break in. Jackie Robinson was the first black baseball player to play major league baseball. Robinson broke the color barrier in baseball with the help of Branch Rickey.

When Banks first came up, he was a shy man but as the years passed he became more comfortable with the writers and reporters. Eventually, he reached the top of his profession when he was inducted into the baseball hall of fame. He had many great quotes and this one has everything to do with life. How many people do you know that are searching for happiness? According to Banks, we should look within ourselves for happiness instead of expecting it from other places. Ernie Banks always came across as a positive thinking person. A man who always had kind things to say. Banks passed away in 2015. A great player and man whose legacy will live forever.

NUMBER 42

"Every strike brings me closer to the next home run."

Babe Ruth

This quote was made when a strike was just a pitch, not something the union recommended to get more money from their owners. Babe Ruth at one time held the record for the most strikeouts and the most Home Runs. This was many years before steroids and free agents entered the game. Babe Ruth played the game in the early 1900's. Before he became the great slugger that he is known for, he was a tremendous left-handed pitcher.

The Babe once called baseball, "the greatest game in the world." Babe Ruth had many nick names, the great Bambino, the Sultan of swat, and the Babe, just to name a few. Some of his teammates called him "Jidge" but his name given by his parents was George Herman Ruth. He passed in 1945, but even today just about everyone has at least heard of Babe Ruth. He was among the first group of players inducted into the baseball hall of fame.

I think what Mr. Ruth was trying to say in this quote is each failure brings us closer to success. Sometime success must be searched for many times before it is reached. Do not ever stop trying to reach your goals in life. It is my belief, everyone can become successful if they only try and never, never give up.

NUMBER 43

"Never blame myself when I'm not hitting. I just blame the bat and if it keeps up, I change bats. After all, if I know it isn't my fault that I'm not hitting, how can I get mad at myself."

Yogi Berra

Yogi Berra was a catcher for the New York Yankees back before steroids, big contracts and free agents dominated the game. He became even more famous many years after his playing career for his acting roles in commercials. Berra also stayed in baseball as both a coach and a manager. He played for the New York Yankees 19 years. Inducted in to the baseball Hall of Fame in 1972, Berra is such an interesting character that he even has a museum in New Jersey.

Probably one of the most quotable athletes of all time known for his most favorite saying; "it ain't over till it's over." I like this quote because he never blames himself which tells me that he is looking at life with a positive twist. Striving for consistency in hitting a baseball can be applied to life. Being consistent helps you achieve goals. Consistency is a solid trait to have. Focus on your goal and be consistent in your approach to achieving it.

NUMBER 44

"I've missed more than 9000 shots in my career. I've lost almost 300 games. 26 times, I've been trusted to take the game winning shot and missed. I've failed over and over and over again in my life. And that is why I succeed."

Michael Jordan

Michael Jordan was arguably the greatest basketball player of all time. I had the opportunity to watch many of his games. I think many of the players believed he was the type of player, if he was on your team you felt as if you had a chance to win every game. In this famous quote, he tells us, in life that is ok to fail. If you fail over and over the average person will probably give up. Jordan exemplifies the attitude of a successful athlete. Although he missed all those shots, and failed in those games, in the end he and his team the Chicago Bulls were able to win six world championships. The Bulls built a statue of Michael Jordan just outside of the United Center, the home of the Chicago Bulls. Without Mr. Jordan the Bulls probably would have never won a championship.

NUMBER 45

"Most important thought, if you love someone, tell him or her, for you never know what tomorrow may have in store."
Walter Payton

This is a great quote from a great athlete who died way before his time. Payton was one of the greatest football players to ever play the game. Similar to Michael Jordan his presence made his team better. He played hard all the time and transformed himself into a great player with his famous off season conditioning program which included running up a hill near his home. Tell the ones you love your true feelings because you never know when the end will arrive. Remember to love and let yourself be loved. Many Chicago Bears fans loved Walter Payton and the way he played the great game of football.

NUMBER 46

"Life is a gamble. You can get hurt, but people die in plane crashes, lose their arms and legs in car accidents; people die every day. Same with fighters: some die, some get hurt, some go on. You just don't let yourself believe it will happen to you."

Muhammad Ali

Muhammad Ali, born under the name Cassius Marcellus Clay on January 17, 1942 in Louisville, Kentucky became the ultimate self promoter of his time and arguably one of the greatest heavy weight boxing champions of all time He won the gold medal in the Olympics in 1959. Ali captured the world's attention in the 1960's when he predicted victory over the then heavily favored boxing champion Sonny Liston. Later in the decade, after he became the boxing champion and during the heat of the Vietnam war, Cassius Clay changed his name to Muhammad Ali. He changed his name and his religion to avoid going to war in Vietnam. Boxing at that time stripped him of his championship title. Ali would later regain the title. Ali said what he wanted and did what he wanted do and at time when civil rights were in turmoil in our country. Just about everyone who followed boxing had respect for Muhammad Ali as a fighter and entertainer.

Life is a gamble. Each day is a blessing and we never know what life holds in store. This uncertainty is part of what makes life so precious.

NUMBER 47

"Every professional athlete owes a debt of gratitude to the fans and management, and pays an installment every time he plays. He should never miss a payment."

Bobby Hull

Bobby Hull was my favorite athlete and in my opinion, the most dominant Hockey player of all time. Back in the day, he was the Michael Jordon of Hockey. He played hard all the time. I shot the puck left handed because of Bobby Hull. He made the game fun to watch and the children of my day admired him, similar to the way Michael Jordon was admired. Tremendous skill, speed, determination, and a wicked slap shot, was the best way to describe Hull.

I agree with this quote. I feel every athlete serves a roll for our young people who love sports and like to play. Athletes, especially today, earn enormous amounts of money to play a child's game. In my opinion, athletes owe it to the children of our world to set examples for the youth. I feel some have failed, but many more have succeeded. No matter what profession you aspire to, we all owe it to the children to set an example because someday we will be gone and the world will belong to the youth of today. My question to you is; how do you want to leave your mark on society? Bobby Hull said it best back the day when he stated this quote.

NUMBER 48

"You've got to love what you're doing. If you love it, you can overcome any handicap or the soreness or all the aches and pains, and continue to play for a long, long time."

Gordie Howe

When I was growing up Gordie Howe was still playing and it seemed he would play forever. He was great Hockey player who played for the Detroit Red Wings. Howe was known as a gentleman in Hockey and a true hockey legend.

I feel that the athletes of Howe's time respected the game and really played for the love of the sport, more than just the money. True athletes that love the game cannot help but play with some degree of pain. In the non sporting world where most of us spend our time, we all work with some pain or sickness. For many people, if they did not work hurt or sick, they may not have a job.

Life is not always easy. Pain and suffering is very much part of life. There are people that overcome handicaps and do things in life that people who seemingly have everything cannot accomplish. Tough people are ones that overcome obstacles and achieve great things in life. Always remember that no matter how bad you are hurt or disabled there is someone who is hurting more than you.

NUMBER 49

"You spend a good piece of your life gripping a baseball and in the end it turns out that it was the other way around all the time".

Jim Bouton

Jim Bouton was not a Hall of Fame pitcher, nor was he known as a great athlete; rather he made his mark with the famous book called "Ball Four." He did have a good knuckleball pitch that kept his career alive.

He was known for his dry humor and if you have never read his book you owe it to yourself to take the time. I feel it is a must read for a true Baseball fan. It is filled with great baseball stories and many of the players at that time became mad at Bouton for writing personal stories about them. His honesty and the humor that he extracted from the great game of baseball is unparalleled

When you really love your occupation, eventually it somehow defines who you are in life. For example if your passion is to become a fireman and you save someone's life from a burning building and it makes all the headlines that is who you are, a heroic fireman. We are defined by our actions in life. We become known for what we do in this world.

NUMBER 50

"Baseball is a red-blooded sport for red-blooded men. It's no pink tea, and mollycoddles had better stay out. It's a struggle for supremacy, a survival of the fittest."

"The great trouble with baseball today is that most of the players are in the game for the money and that's it, not for the love of it, the excitement of it, the thrill of it."

Ty Cobb

I saved one of the best character athletes quotes for last. One of the toughest and greatest hitters of all time was Ty Cobb. He was so famous they made a movie about his life after his death in 1960. He played with a chip on his shoulder and was hated by many.

The first quote sums up the way Cobb approached the game. It was said that he used to sharpen his spikes to make the infielders fear him when he would slide into the base. There are many stories about this colorful baseball player who starred in the game in the early 1900's.

I originally had only one quote from Cobb but, when I read the second one, I thought it needs to be in this book because it confirms the way I feel about some of today's athletes. If Ty Cobb were alive today, I wonder what he would have said about the money being paid to professional athletes today. To say the least, his opinion would have been interesting.

Notes

_____

_____

_____

_____

_____

_____

_____

_____

The Philosophers

These are the quotes from philosophers and for this chapter there need not be an introduction, just the words.

"It is twenty-four centuries since Socrates walked through the market place of Athens".

"The human world has changed almost beyond recognition. In everything that pertains to man's act and accomplishments, in technology, in social institutions, in the very face of the earth, there is change. Yet in man himself, we find deep continuities which link us to Socrates' world. Men are still speculative, still reflective. They still wonder about the limits and meaning of the universe, they still heed Socrates' call to reflect upon the fundamental principles of thought and action. Because of this continuity in man's nature over more than two millennia, philosophy has never forgotten its past. It is appropriate, therefore, that we should approach the subject of philosophy through a reading of some of the great works of the philosophical tradition."

Robert Paul Wolfe
1969

NUMBER 51

"He is richest who is content with the least, for content is the wealth of nature."

Socrates

The Greek philosopher Socrates was born in 469 BC and died in 399 BC. His quotes and wisdom are famous and as I stated in the books introduction he is the reason I became interested in quotes and philosophy in general.

Being rich is not just about money but rather about a lifestyle and an attitude. You do not need to be rich to be content, although it may help. When you are rich, you should have content. Many people I meet that are wealthy seem to share this contentment, however not all of them. It is something everyone should strive for. If you really think about life in general, which is what philosophy makes us do, we only need food and water to exist. Everything else, our homes, money, cars, and all material things are things that man created for us all to enjoy are just used while we live. To what degree you enjoy them is a direct reflection of how bad you want these things. True wealth is in the beauty that is in everyone and in nature.

NUMBER 52

"Human behavior flows from three main sources: desire, emotion, and knowledge."

Plato

The great Greek philosopher Plato was born in 427 BC and died in 347 BC. He was the man who studied under Socrates and became a famous philosopher through the years.

This quote makes so much sense when you break it down. Behavior, the way we act is because of what we want, the desire, how we feel, our emotion, and how we proceed about our business and our knowledge really define who we are as a human being.

NUMBER 53

"Wise men speak because they have something to say; Fools because they have to say something."

Plato

I liked this quote because of the profoundness of it. Speak when you have something to say, is that not what we teach our children at a young age? How many times have you told your child not to speak? We raise our children to grow up wise yet there seems to be a lack of wisdom in our society today. This quote should be posted on all billboards across America. Maybe that would change the world or at least what we say.

NUMBER 54

"A man in a fit of anger is actuated in a very different manner from one who only thinks of that emotion."

David Hume

David Hume lived from 1711 until 1776. He is considered by many as the greatest philosopher to write in the English language. The information and this quote came directly from the Robert Paul Wolff' book titled, "Ten Great Works of Philosophy."

Hume wrote and studied the theory and philosophy on human nature. This quote came directly from his writings called "Inquiries."

This quote reinforces my feeling that a person can think whatever they want. Remember the old saying, "Actions speak louder than words?" I have always thought that a person can have thoughts, however to act on their thoughts is very different. You can think for free but sometimes you have to pay for your actions.

NUMBER 55

"Be strong and of a good courage, Act for the best, hope for the best, and take what comes. If death ends all, we cannot meet death better."

William James

William James was considered a modern philosopher. He lived from 1842 until 1910. James was a remarkable man. He had impeccable credentials. He was a psychologist, doctor, student of comparative religion, and a philosopher. He also taught at the Harvard medical school and later in his life taught philosophy there. This quote sounds like the basis for positive thinking. Build yourself up take care of your mind and body, try not to stress out over what you cannot control and when you die you will have done your best. Sounds like a philosophy for life. Have no regrets in life and hurt no one.

NUMBER 56

"Those who educate children well are more to be honoured than they who produce them; for these only gave them life, those the art of living well."

Aristotle

It is very important in today's world to educate our children. After all, children are the future of the world. Many people can be a parent, however it takes someone special to take the time to educate their children. What are you teaching your children? In today's fast paced world, there are many situations where both parents are either divorced or working full time. The people that suffer the most in these situations are always the children.

Aristotle said it well all those years ago and it is still true today. Teach our children but teach them well.

NUMBER 57

"Nothing is given to man on earth - struggle is built into the nature of life, and conflict is possible - the hero is the man who lets no obstacle prevent him from pursuing the values he has chosen."

Andrew Bernstein

Bernstein is an American philosopher born in 1949. I like his quote because it is a very bold view on life. It is true that a hero is someone who does not let obstacles get in the way of being great or doing great things.

Life is very much a struggle. Animals struggle in the wild and humans struggle in society. There is conflict everywhere in life. People struggle with their lives, their jobs, their health, their relationships, and their own worlds. Life has no magic formula. Everyone needs to figure things out by themselves or be fortunate to have a great mentor.

NUMBER 58

"All that really belongs to us is time; even he who has nothing else has that."

Baltasar Gracian

Baltasar Gracian was born in 1883. He remained so firmly dedicated to democracy that he shot himself rather than surrender to police. This is interesting because he actually took his time away from himself as he died for his beliefs.

I relate this quote to the song earlier by the band, Chicago. Does anybody really know what time it is? All we really have in this world is time and it is limited. People all choose to use their time in their own way. Some people become rich and some are homeless. The interesting question I get from this is why some people seem to have all the time in the world, while other people never seem to have any. Yet as we know, it is all the same for everyone. Use your time wisely because some day the clock of life will end.

NUMBER 59

"Every book is a quotation; and every house is a quotation out of all forests, and mines, and stone quarries; and every man is a quotation from all his ancestors."

Ralph Waldo Emerson

Ralph Waldo Emerson was thought of as a wonderful poet and a philosopher in his time. He was born in 1803 and passed in 1882. Emerson led the transcendentalist movement of the 19th century. He has produced many quotes which I enjoy. I found this one interesting because he is saying that almost everything is a quote. Maybe what he meant was that everything such as a home, a book, or a person represents something and something can be said about each one. If you had to use one or two quotes to describe yourself, what would they be?

NUMBER 60

"Write it on your heart that every day is the best day in the year."

Ralph Waldo Emerson

What a wonderful quote. Emerson came up with another beauty. If you felt in your heart that everyday was always the best day of the year, that each day was better than the last, you might never have a bad day. If everyone had that feeling in their heart each day, imagine how much greater life would be? How much happier would you be? How much more productive would you be? Remember in the beginning when I asked those five questions? Perhaps this is the key to finding those answers.

Notes

_____

_____

_____

_____

_____

_____

_____

_____

The Writers

Where would we be today if no one had ever written a book? What if no person ever put their thoughts to paper? If you have ever written a book or short story, you know it takes time and much thought. There are thousands of wonderful writers and so many great quotes to choose from.

We never know when another great writer will emerge from the ranks of obscurity, but it is inevitable that many will certainly find their way and place in history. Books are education in the purest form. It is true many people rely only on the internet for information, however the real truths are in the books. Many times internet information is not 100% accurate. A written book, especially a college textbook is information and knowledge that has been researched and edited. I encourage everyone to read books even if it is in electronic form. Reading expands your mind and gives you tremendous knowledge above and beyond anything else. I can always tell when I am speaking to an educated person. Usually educated people portray confidence and sincere knowledge.

Please take the time to read. I always encouraged my children to read. Set aside time everyday to read whatever it is you are interested in. Do this for a year and you will be amazed at how much smarter you will become. You will find that new interests will appear and hopefully you will become excited about learning more.

I hope you will enjoy the ten quotes from our world's great writers.

NUMBER 61

"All my life I've looked at words as though I were seeing them for the first time."

Ernest Hemingway

Ernest Hemingway, born in 1899, is one of the most famous American writers of the 20th century. He wrote novels and short stories about outdoorsmen, soldiers and other men of action, and his plainspoken no-frills writing style became so famous that it was (and still is) frequently parodied. Although he was born in Oak Park, Illinois, he lived in Paris, Cuba, and Key West. He served as a war correspondent in WWII and the Spanish Civil War. Hemingway sealed his own notoriety when he killed himself with a shotgun in 1961.

I like this quote because it gives us a fresh approach to writing. What a great way to approach writing. A simple thought, almost similar to a baby seeing the world for the first time.

NUMBER 62

"I'm no politician. I'm a historian who has learned through a lifetime of studying that nothing in the world beats universal education."

Stephen Ambrose

Ambrose was born in 1936. He wrote about historic wars and was very interested in history, mainly historic battles. He wrote a few books about Eisenhower as well. He died in 2002.

There is much truth to this quote. Education is very important to the future of our country. If everyone in the world were given an equal opportunity to educate themselves, what a better world this would be. Imagine if everyone was able to be educated to the top of their particular level of learning, how wonderful the world would be. Today the costs associated with higher education are too great for many people to obtain. Learn as much as you possibly can and you will never regret it.

NUMBER 63

"Life would be infinitely happier if we could only be born at the age of eighty and gradually approach eighteen."

Mark Twain

Mark Twain was born in 1835 and passed in 1910. He was famous for his books The Adventures of Huckleberry Finn and The Adventures of Tom Sawyer. He became an influence on many great writers with his great wit and humor.

Wouldn't that be something if we could live life in reverse? Getting the older years out of the way and getting younger each day. Every day the pain would diminish a little more. The wrinkles would straighten out as if an iron was put to them. Just think how much you would know when you reached the age of 25. The imagination of a writer is portrayed in this quote.

NUMBER 64

"As a single footstep will not make a path on the earth, so a single thought will not make a pathway in the mind. To make a deep physical path, we walk again and again. To make a deep mental path, we must think over and over the kind of thoughts we wish to dominate our lives."

Henry David Thoreau

Thoreau was born in 1817 and passed in 1862. He wrote some books that are similar to the self help books of today. One book he wrote was called, "Happiness."

This quote says to us that we become what we think about. The thoughts that we put in our head dominate our lives. Isn't it important to feed our minds good positive thoughts? If you practice this habit day after day a person can accomplish almost anything they set their mind to. We have a choice each day what kind of thoughts go into our minds. The choices that we make can really have an influence on what happens to us throughout our lives. Think well and wellness will come. Think great and greatness will appear.

NUMBER 65

"I am only one, but still I am one. I cannot do everything, but still I can do something; and because I cannot do everything, I will not refuse to do something that I can do."

Helen Keller

Helen Keller was born in 1880 and lived until 1968. She was the first deaf blind person to earn a bachelor of arts degree. She was a famous author, political activist and lecturer. She left us with many wonderful quotes and it was difficult for me to pick one. I like this one because it takes the things we do and makes them simple. Just do something that you can do as it is better than doing nothing at all. This woman accomplished so much in her life while being not able to see or hear. A true inspiration to everyone.

NUMBER 66

"Except a living man there is nothing more wonderful than a book! A message to us from the dead - from human souls we never saw, who lived, perhaps, thousands of miles away. And yet these, in those little sheets of paper, speak to us, arouse us, terrify us, teach us, comfort us, open their hearts to us as brothers."

Charles Kingsley

Charles Kingsley was born in 1819 and passed in 1875. He was from Devonshire, England. Kingsley was a priest, a professor and a novelist. He also wrote fairy tales for children in his later years. This quote has a dramatic feel to it. It speaks of his passion for reading and writing. It is true there are so many things to learn from a book. We read books from people that lived in different times in history. We read books from modern writers. The magic is that they all have something to say. All we need to do is open them up and listen to them with our minds. Open up the world of reading and you open up the world of thought.

NUMBER 67

"Once we believe in ourselves, we can risk curiosity, wonder, spontaneous delight, or any experience that reveals the human spirit."

E.E. Cummings

Edward Estlin Cummings was an American poet born in 1894 and passed in 1968. He was known as an eccentric in his time. This quote is true because in order to achieve happiness and success, you must believe in yourself. When you believe in yourself, it gives you confidence and the ability to experience life without some of the uncertainties and insecurities that accompany not believing in yourself. This again is a very positive quote that gives me an uplifting feeling.

NUMBER 68

"Stress is basically a disconnection from the earth, a forgetting of the breath. Stress is an ignorant state. It believes that everything is an emergency. Nothing is that important. Just lie down."

"Trust in what you love, continue to do it, and it will take you where you need to go."

Natalie Goldberg

Natalie Goldberg was born in 1948. She has put out many books to teach and inspire future writers. She is also an excellent speaker. I like her two quotes because they both make so much sense to me. We all feel stress at one point or another in our lives. It is true that when you feel stress it is best to just slow down, take a deep breath and try to relax. This quote, I believe, was inspired from her studies of Zen, the personal expression of human incite, for over twenty years.

The next quote is about trusting in love. It sounds like the Beatles could have written it. Love will take you where you want to go, or as she says where you need to go.

NUMBER 69

"Do we need to have 280 brands of breakfast cereal? No, probably not. But we have them for a reason - because some people like them. It's the same with baseball statistics."

Bill James

    Bill James has written books on baseball statistics and the history of the game. He has changed the way baseball is viewed today. If you are a follower of the game of baseball, then you are probably a fan of numbers and baseball history. It has been said that baseball is a game of numbers. It has also been called a thinking man's game. His thought is the old statistics such as batting average and home runs are not a true indication of a players talent. What he believes is how can a player make his team win more games. After all the most important stat in baseball, is winning baseball games. Baseball is a team sport decided by individual human results.

    In this quote he refers to the many brands of cereal, comparing them to the many stats in baseball. Everybody has their favorites. We have more brands because somebody probably likes each one.

NUMBER 70

"Every man's life ends the same way. It is only the details of how he lived and how he died that distinguish one man from another."

Ernest Hemingway

I thought I would end this chapter as it began with a Hemingway quote. It is true that men are set apart by what they do with their lives. Some men go on and accomplish great things in life while others accomplish little. The details of a person's life are usually filled with many events, however only that person has the ability to create them. What are your accomplishments in life? Do you ever wonder what people will say about you when you leave this earth?

Notes

_____

_____

_____

_____

_____

_____

_____

_____

Everyday People

These are us the readers and the writers. The engineers and the plumbers. The electricians and the teachers. The barbers and the beauticians. The people that live life and are all just looking to survive. We all may want a little more than we have in life, or maybe we are satisfied with who we are and what we have become. Anyone can be that every day person. What this chapter is about is very simple. I asked for quotes from people that I either know have known for many years or from people that I only met one time. The response I received from all was very positive and the everyday people were happy to help. We all want to belong to something and now these people will live in memory as long as this book stays in print. Maybe in some way I brought a little happiness to these people that helped me write this book of quotes. Most of the friends and family remained anonymous for privacy reason. The names are only revealed if they gave me their permission. Either way I thank them and am thrilled to have them become part of this. I hope they feel the same way.

NUMBER 71

"He who hesitates, loses out"

My Uncle who wishes to remain Anonymous

This speaks loud and clear from someone who as of this writing is living well into his 70's. This person has been around and seen many different places and things. Lost opportunity may never come back again. If we act on opportunities when they occur, even if we fail at least we can feel as though we tried. How many times have you had a great idea and never acted on it. The world is filled with lost opportunity and lost hope. How bad do you want it? If you want something figure out how to go out and get it. My uncle is a living book of knowledge and he probably could have come up with over a hundred quotes by himself. I am grateful that he offered this one to us. This quote should be in every motivational publication that discusses procrastination. This is what keeps us from doing what we want and getting the things in life that we all deserve. Hesitation is parallel to procrastination. Hesitating, prolonging, waiting until suddenly the chance or opportunity is gone. Remember it is never too late to follow your dreams.

NUMBER 72

"Most of life's negotiable issues are proportional, pre-determined or unfair."

Richard J. Budziak

This is from a man who was taught well by his father, who had a strong character and was a world war II hero. I've known Rich for many years and he has always been a positive influence in my life. I am proud to call him my friend. His quote makes you realize that you make your way in the world. Life has its deposits and withdrawals. When we negotiate something many times we are trying to gain an advantage. Negotiating is important because you are trying to satisfy needs of both parties involved. Buy the car you want and pay the price you want to pay. One of your choices may change. You may pay a little more for the car or you may not get exactly all the features you want on the car. This would bring proportion to the deal. Pre-determined is different. This may be an example of something you want but the price is not negotiable and a determination must be met as to whether or not you really want to make the purchase. All in all this is an interesting quote from an interesting man who has a solid positive outlook on life.

NUMBER 73

"Don't play Russian Roulette with your nest egg."

Anonymous

Several years ago I was giving a presentation at one of the local libraries. It was a wonderful crowd and I asked if anyone would be interested in participating in my book of quote's. Everyone was very eager to participate. This quote was said well before the economy took a turn for the worse. It was almost a prediction of what one should realize eventually. I suppose as you get older it is important to conserve what you have worked so hard to accumulate. Protect your assets and all that important stuff. The real message may be to make wise decisions with your hard earned dollars because if you lose them they are gone and you may have to work twice as hard to replace what you once had. It seems as we get older we slow down. When that phenomenon occurs and I think it is different in everyone, there is a tenancy to hold on to what we have. Others seem to want to give everything away. I suppose it depends on our mental state. It is a strange time in life. I think it is a time when a person starts to realize that the days are numbered and they have come to the end of the journey. That is why it is important to live in the moment and be grateful for your life.

NUMBER 74

"So they say whoever controls the past, controls the future."

Anonymous

I'm not sure who told me this one but I jotted it down on some small piece of paper and kept it on my desk. I looked at it several times and thought about what this meant. My interpretation is that what we did in the past somehow molds what we become in the future. If you start out young and have direction in your life by knowing what you want to become, you may reach your goal of becoming that person. When we are young, despite what are parents tell us, we make decisions. Those decisions determine in many ways what our future becomes. Think about this: you work hard at school and maybe you love to sing and are gifted with a great singing voice. Someone suggests to you that a career as a singer would be almost impossible to have. So the person makes a life changing decision not to become a singer and instead chooses another occupation. The past controlled the future. The same can be said of a tragic accident. One tragic accident may control the future of a person. What is in your past that may be holding you back?

NUMBER 75

"The road to a friend's house is never long."

Anonymous

A nice simple saying that says so much. How many of us really have true friends that we can't wait to see. Many of us have old friends that we haven't seen for years because our lives just change. Maybe this quote will motivate you to go visit that good friend that you think about fondly but hardly ever get to talk to or see. The experience may enhance your life to the point that it may influence you to do something you always wanted to but for some reason never did. When you find a good friend, do all you can to help that person and be a good friend in return. This is the special part of life, the part that really makes life worth living. The wonderful relationships that we share with each other. Lasting relationships that are enjoyable by both people are probably some of the most special things in life. The sad part is that all good things do not last forever, however, enjoy the ride because it is this journey that helps bring happiness. Interacting with other people is very important in life.

NUMBER 76

"Make all you can, save all you can, and love all you can."
Anonymous friend

This is from someone who always thinks about other people almost to a fault. If you make all you can this can be interpreted as artistic or materialistic, either way it is a very positive point of view. Save all you can puts that eye on the future which is so important. Tomorrow comes without much warning. Are you prepared? Are you ready for love? Do you give love as well as you receive it? I think the whole world needs more love in it and if everyone loved all they could, what a wonderful world this would be. It think Art Garfunkel said that among many others. This could probably be a slogan for some advertisement. I suppose just do all you can and save all you can and then just love until your life is over.

NUMBER 77

"Not by age but by capacity is wisdom acquired."

Anonymous friend

Some people are old in number but not wise in age. They may have aged but have little wisdom. That's just the way it is. How much are you willing to learn? How much do you yearn for knowledge? We all exist but how do you want to live? By expanding your knowledge and learning many different things it is possible to stumble into wisdom and have deep thoughts that have meaning to you. Think about some decisions that were made pertaining to our country. Decisions to pass certain laws, declaring war on other countries, and tax code changes. We may find out later in history if these were wise decisions. I'm quite sure that the men that make these decisions thought they were wise ones at the time, or did they? We can only hope, the leaders we elect have our best interests at the forefront of large impacting decisions.

NUMBER 78

"You should try to be happy about everything and not try to do things just to become happy."

Anonymous

I think what she means is that some people try to make themselves happy by buying things or paying for entertainment. And although, this may create happiness it is only for a short time. Eventually you will need more things or more entertainment that will never be enough. We as humans create our own happiness in our own minds. Is it real happiness or is it something made up in our minds. If we try to take things in stride and live and love maybe happiness will just unfold in our lives. A happy person is usually a successful one.

NUMBER 79

"What is one man's meat is another man's poisons. What is good for one is not always good for another."

Bob Mahoney

This quote came from a lecture I gave several years ago at a small library in the south suburbs of Chicago, Illinois. This gentleman was kind enough to write it down and I kept the paper until now. I liked this quote because it says that even though we are all humans we have different likes and dislikes. Knowing that is OK. We do not have to all agree but we should all try to get along. This quote is probably one of the reasons there are so many brands and flavors of toothpaste and cereal. Life is loaded with choices, yet sometimes it seems as though our choices are limited in certain situations. This kind of reminds me of garbage. When you put something out for the garbage man to take and you know it still has value but you let it go anyway. I always imagine that some person finds this thing and just thinks it is the best thing he or she has ever found. One man's junk is another mans treasure.

NUMBER 80

"Measure accomplishment not activity; because it's not the doing that matters, it's what gets done."

Anonymous

Here is a man that is looking for results in life. The truth is that many people spin their wheels making the same mistakes over and over and wonder why they do not get the results they hoped to achieve. Someone once told me the definition of insanity is doing the same thing over and over but expecting different results. This quote goes along side of goal setting. Results are really what dictate what someone becomes. For instance, Michael Jordan is known as a champion mainly because he led the Chicago Bulls to six World Championships in the 1990's. If Jordan had not won all those championships, he may not have the same reputation as he does today. When you accomplish something in life, your mark is made and you forever become associated with that accomplishment. In life, we are constantly taking on new tasks. Some may have more importance to us than others, but ultimately we are trying to get things done. It is this feeling of accomplishment that drives us to complete our work or accomplish goals.

Notes

_____

_____

_____

_____

_____

_____

_____

_____

Old Sayings

These old sayings are common phrases or quotes that have been said for years. The origins are unknown to me, but some are said and heard almost on a daily basis and to give any individual credit for them would seem almost unfair. These old sayings belong to everyone. I've heard these over the years and many times I'll say one and the person next to me will say one I haven't heard for awhile. You may use these old sayings and maybe you will read one that is unfamiliar to you. They are yours to have and to hold.

It may be true that some of these sayings have a negative connotation, however we must remember where they came from. They probably began when times were tough. They are old sayings and many years ago people struggled just to put food on the table. Our times will bring old sayings to our future. Times change as does society and the systems that make up our world. As these changes come to fruition and pass, new sayings will be born. Remember the sixties when some young people said they were feeling groovy?

Can you think of any that are not here? Take the challenge and see if you can come up with 10 of your own. Use this at a party. This can be a game. Pick the old sayings that are not already in this book. A prize can be awarded to the person that comes up with the most. Select a panel of judges of your choice to decide which ones are your best. Go ahead and take the old saying challenge. Every generation seems to come up with a saying, a hip phrase that someday will be an old saying. I hope you dig them.

NUMBER 81

"A penny saved is a penny earned"

Unknown

I wanted to start with this one because of my background. Actually, this is what I have been teaching people to do for years, save their money. We never know what we will need in the future. We preach this to our children. The more pennies we have, the more comfortable our lives will be. Let's do the math. If we saved a penny an hour, that would be only 24 in a day. Do this for 25 five years and you would have 219,000 pennies or $2,190.00. Now if you multiplied that out and saved 100 pennies a day for 25 years, which is only a dollar a day, you would have $9,125.00. This may not be much but I heard somewhere that the average American over 50 years old has less than $10,000.00 saved for their retirement. Imagine if you saved more. This is the reason parents preach to their children about the importance of saving money. My great Aunt used to say, "it's not what you make, it's what you save." Although a penny is only one hundredth of one dollar, it still is a penny. I used to know a guy, when I was in high school, who used to always look on the ground for money. I must have seen this one guy find hundreds of pennies in the few years that I knew him. We would walk to the baseball game or walk home from school and he was always finding pennies. Perhaps you used to do this or maybe you knew someone just like my old friend.

NUMBER 82

"Don't be penny wise and dollar foolish."

Unknown

This is an interesting quote probably dating back to the great depression starting in the late 1920's in the United States. It means to me that if you try to save a small amount of money that's fine, however, really do your homework before parting with a large amount of money. Being dollar foolish is a great way to get into debt problems. I had a great aunt that passed several years ago. Her life was dedicated to her mother and providing financially. She worked hard her whole life. Without any formal college education, she acquired a job and became as dedicated to her employer as she was to her mother. I remember her using this quote quite often and consequently it must have stuck in my head.

NUMBER 83

"Good friends are hard to find."

Unknown

How many times has this been said? When a predicament occurs or a bad situation involving someone who you thought was your friend, the person let you down and was not really your friend. Most people are fortunate and should consider themselves grateful to have two or three really good friends. Many people have many friends but how many are really good friends. Good friends are similar to gold. Gather your friends as if you were starting a charity. Who do you want around you that always thinks of others first? Everyone admires a person who puts themselves last and others first. Good friends will listen to your problems. They will bring you up when you are down. They will make sense of the things that don't make sense to you. Good friends are honest and trustworthy. They don't tell you what you want to hear but they reinforce what the real truth is. A good friend is someone that doesn't look at the clock constantly but wants to spend time with you because you are part of their time. We should all try to be good friends to someone. Try our hardest not to judge others. Try to make relationships the ones that you will never forget. These great relationships will make you happy and bring fulfillment to your life. Everyone should love people because deep down we are all the same.

NUMBER 84

"A friend in need is a friend indeed."

Unknown

Everybody needs somebody sometime. The late great Dean Martin wrote that song and it goes hand in hand with this quote. When we need a friend, those that are fortunate, have someone to whom they can turn to. A shoulder to cry on or sometimes just someone to listen to us vent our problems or frustrations. Life can be very difficult and lonely to live with no friends around. As we all know from the previous quote, a good friend is the best. Maybe to take it a step further we can say that we find out who our real friends are in times of trouble. This is when a real friend is needed. If you go through life and have only a few real close friends consider yourself very fortunate. If you are a fortunate person then try to treat your close friends like gold because most times they are as golden as life can be.

NUMBER 85

"Don't count your chickens before they're hatched."

Unknown

When we expect things to happen and they don't, it opens the door for disappointment. Try not to expect things to always work out as planned. In fact, life is full of disappointment. The key is not to let it get you down. If we are grateful in life, then, everything good that happens to us makes us that much more happier. When a setback occurs, it may be because you were counting on something and expecting it to happen. It is quite possible that this quote evolved with actual chickens. The egg never hatched so you couldn't count the chicken. Even if that is true, it can still motivate us if we allow it and not expecting anything extra until it comes to fruition. Always take the approach to expect nothing and when something good occurs it should excite you. After all, isn't excitement next to happiness?

NUMBER 86

"You're only as young as you feel."

Unknown

How do you feel? Do you hurt or do you feel like you are the king or queen of the hill? As you read this you are ageing, in fact, from the moment we are born we are on our way to dying. Now that sounds pretty depressing. Take care of yourself, eat right, exercise, and avoid smoking. Get an annual physical after you become an adult and control your weight. These tips will help you feel young. That's really a huge part of what life is, how we feel or how we view the world. One thing that is for certain is that most people can control their thoughts if they try. What thoughts do you have each day? Are they the ones that make you feel young? Remember, you can feel as young as you allow yourself to feel. Take control of your life. It starts by controlling your thoughts and how you feel about yourself. Be your best friend.

NUMBER 87

"Laugh and the whole world laughs with you, cry and you cry alone."

Unknown

When we are in a good mood sometimes it affects the people around us and almost inspires others. Conversely, the opposite is also true. Laughing is great therapy for people that are ill. Everyone should make an effort to laugh at least once every day. The world provides plenty of things to laugh at each day. The comedians and clowns try to make us laugh. It is not really that hard to find laughter, it is all around. Make a conscious effort to laugh everyday and inspire those people you know to try and do the same. Don't be the one that stands alone. Laugh and be happy or cry and be sad. Sometimes things happen and there is nothing we can do except accept the feeling. Everyone cries sometime and everyone laughs sometimes. Try to laugh more and you will probably feel more happiness.

NUMBER 88

"The best laid plans of mice and men."

Unknown

Many people have big dreams and sometimes they to fade away in time. It does not mean that we should give up hope or stop dreaming, but rather keep moving forward. If our plans fail, well, the reason may have been beyond our control. Just chalk it up to fate. Sometimes things just happen. We may never even find the reason or the reason may not be clear in that particular moment. Making plans is a wonderful part of life. Many people make new plans every day. To me this is living life. Some would argue that it is more fun to just venture into life without making plans and just find out where it goes. If you live that way and are happy then it works for you. Living and doing things in the spur of the moment can be fun. Enjoying the adventure is certainly an exciting way to live. John Lennon said in one of his songs, "life is what happens to you while you're busy making other plans."

NUMBER 89

"It's not the size of the dog in the fight, but the size of the fight in the dog?"

Unknown

The old David vs. Goliath theory. Many years ago, Sam Wyly tried to purchase Western Union and was turned down. Wyly refers to this quote in his book, "1,000 Dollars and an Idea." Many great people have accomplished great feats without seemingly having a chance. Sports are filled with such stories. A great Sports story of recent years are the Los Angeles Kings in the NHL. They won the Stanley cup after just barely making the playoffs and being the last seed. Great battles in history were won when the victor had no chance in the beginning. The underdog sometimes prevails. There are beautiful times when the underdog wins.

NUMBER 90

"If it isn't broke then don't fix it"

Unknown

A pretty simple saying but how many times have we tried to fix something that is not broke. I remember early in my insurance career we had what were called, "prospecting ideas." The idea worked well but we got bored or tired of the same thing so we would change things and then a good idea turned into one that would not work anymore. As simple as the saying is remember to fix what is broke and leave what is working alone. Do not fix something until it needs fixing.

Notes

_____

_____

_____

_____

_____

_____

_____

_____

The Authors Quotes

In this chapter, I will offer you the quotes that I have thought or dreamed of myself. Many are designed just for this book while others are ones I have carried around for years. There is one from a column I wrote for 3 years. It was a weekly column for a local Suburban Chicago newspaper that reached over a million subscribers. Unfortunately, "The Dailey South-town Economist" newspaper exists no longer.

This is the final chapter in this book, and I hope you have enjoyed it. Please look these last ten over and feel free to use them yourself. It is my hope and dream that some people can use these quotes to change their life and make it better. Or as the Beatles once wrote and sang in the classic song, "Hey Jude," "take a sad song and make it better." Even if you're a happy person, remember we all need inspiration. My hope is that one of these quotes in this book will inspire you to change your life in a positive direction. If you are satisfied with what you read please pass it on to someone you know who needs a little enlightenment. After you finish the book, you may want to make up some quotes personal to you and may help you in your journey through life. Please never stop using your creative juices. Creativity is so important in the world.

This is the first of many inspirational and motivational books I have planned for the near future. I say near future, remember this took only 5 years to finish. In my upcoming work, I will try to address finding happiness in your life, struggling through difficult times such as divorce, surviving through a major illness and changing your life to make it better. These are just a few of the topics I plan on addressing in the future.

Thank you very much for reading this book and I am very grateful that you took the time to do so. I hope you have enjoyed reading it as much as I did writing it. Again, thank you.

NUMBER 91

"Try not to dwell on the past because it may make you feel older."

As we should all know, it is always best to live in the present. The reason is because that is our reality. The present time is all we really have for certain. Life can change in a New York minute. If you spend too much time living in the past, it takes your mind off now and will only make you age while sacrificing the present time. Even if the past had some great moments, unforgettable ones, it still does little good to linger in it. Use these past memories to reminisce with friends and family or instead create new unforgettable moments. I heard it said many times that we should learn from the past which is certainly true, however, we should learn and move on. If you like to dwell on moments then try to train your mind to dwell on positive events and try to create positive moments for the here and now.

NUMBER 92

"All human beings make mistakes. The size of the mistake sometimes may determine our destiny."

If you say you never made a mistake then you must be super human. I don't even have any idea how many mistakes I've made. Fortunately, they have kept me on the honest side of the law. It can be very difficult to make life changing decisions, such as starting a new career or beginning to pursue a masters degree. These are choices we make and some turn out good for people and some not so good. I know that if I hadn't attended a certain party, which I was somewhat reluctant at the time due to various reasons, I never would have met the Love of My Life. She feels the same way as she was also reluctant to attend that historic night in our lives. So it is written here that our fate or destiny was determined that memorable night. This fortunately was not a mistake. What if either one of us decided against attending the party? The gist of the quote is try to think very carefully before making any important decisions in your life. One mistake could cost you your life. Repeated mistakes may alter your life forever. The question that comes from this quote is: Are you aware of your mistakes and can you correct them in time to allow a positive impact to occur?

NUMBER 93

"When you are seeking self change it is important to surround yourself with people that make you feel good."

I thought of this quote because of a difficult situation. I wanted to change the situation, however, it became difficult when I saw same faces day in and day out and they were part of the situation I was attempting to separate myself from. The older one gets the harder self improvement becomes. The old saying, "you can't teach an old dog new tricks come to mind." Those same familiar faces may not understand the changes you may want to make. Surrounding yourself with new faces gives you somewhat of a fresh start. It is easier to change your life when you have new influences. These influences or influential people should give you positive feedback or make you feel good about yourself or you may need to seek new company to keep.

NUMBER 94

"Sometimes when the flu knocks you down for a day, your body needs rest but your mind can still dream and think of feeling better."

Well I guess you figured I thought of this when I was sick. I was so sick I couldn't get out of the bed. Weak, sore muscles, it was the basic flu. I used this time to try to get something positive on paper and let me tell you it was hard to do. It felt like the whole world just stopped and left me there in bed. How can someone sick motivate anyone? Well, for those of you that have been real sick, it is real hard to stay positive. So if you take anything from this quote, remember that no matter how sick you are, there is always someone that is feeling worse than you. Use that to get yourself better. No matter how bad or hurt or sick you are, there is always someone that is suffering more in the world. All you need to do is read stories or talk to people and you will find someone who has suffered more.

NUMBER 95

"Divinity derived from the Latin word divinus, is all around us and sometimes within us."

Divinity is a word I always liked. Striving to be divine or God-like is very difficult trait to have and certainly not seen in most humans. I think maybe you get that feeling of divinity when you do something heroic or special. With that being written, there are many people in this world who seek the wisdom and the knowledge to get to that plateau in life. For those of you out there that live a life of divinity, I admire you. Divinity is a beautiful word and it is really a promotion of love. Someone told me just the other day that she dreamed of a giant ball of love and she dove into it. She woke up with a feeling of total freedom and happiness that she had never felt before. Think about that, a giant ball of love.

NUMBER 96

"The worst choice you can make is to do nothing. Nothing leads to nowhere and nowhere is someplace no one wants to go."

This is a quote I wrote several years ago for the Dailey South-town Economist newspaper in the south suburban Chicago area. It was told to me by my editor and chief that the paper had over 1 million subscribers at that time. Now like many newspapers, it no longer exists. I really enjoyed writing that column each week. The column was called "money matters." To me money really does matter but what I enjoy the most is motivating people to take action in their lives and make them better. When I thought of the title for the column and later my radio show, I was trying to motivate readers and listeners to take action with their financial lives. Now, years later, I begin a new phase of my career where I will attempt to motivate individuals to make themselves better people. By better, I simply mean happy. Achieving what it is they truly want from life. Doing what they want in life. My next book will begin that phase in my career. I will attempt to explain in detail how to get almost anything you want in life and be happy.

NUMBER 97

"Time is something that no person owns but rather time owns people."

This is a quote that I actually dreamed about, although in the dream I could not figure out what it meant. When I awoke, I wrote this down and altered it somewhat. If you realize what many people say for instance, "I don't have time for that." or, "I just can't find the time." If you think about it, everyone has the same amount of time in a day, an hour is an hour and a minute is a minute. It is how we spend our time that is loaned to us for free that determines our lives. Why is one man wildly successful and seems to be able to do all kinds of things when his friend can't seem to find time to tie his shoes? They have the same amount of time, however, it is how they manage time that produces the results. So the next time you think you don't have time, you are right you only borrow it for free. A famous comedian once said, "Live every day as if it were your last because someday you will be right."

NUMBER 98

"Life's everyday challenges can become opportunities to enhance your life."

If your life is smooth and not filled with drama, you may be content. Most people face challenges in their lives. It is wiser to face challenges head on and solve day to day problems rather than to avoid them. The reason I say this is because when you solve a problem or face a challenging situation, it puts your mind to work. When your mind is focused, it is in a healthy state. Just remember to learn from the challenge and try not to let it cause you unneeded stress. Every challenge can be turned into an opportunity to grow as a person. The next time you face a challenging situation do not complain but rather welcome it and use it as an opportunity to enhance your life with the experience.

NUMBER 99

"Making a big change in life can be frightening, however what scares me more is regret."

This quote can be apply to almost anyone who lives. We make big changes all the time. For example: buying a home, starting a new career, getting a divorce, and, most especially, having a child. Whatever is important enough for you to do in your life remember this: If you do not welcome that big change in life, you may regret it later. For example, let's say you wanted to start a business. You have a great idea and a great product to sell but you do not seek the funding or whatever it is to start that business. You may regret it the rest of your life. It can tear you up and constantly eat away at your mind. Especially, when you see that similar idea or product being made successfully by someone else. Take a chance in life you only get one and make the changes necessary to make you happy. Do not grow old and bitter because of regrets in life.

NUMBER 100

If we believe that the world is in us and we roam this earth similar to the dinosaurs of years past, then why can we not make earth, our home, the greatest gift of all time?

As you can read this is not a quote. This question is challenging you for the answer. The reason is because we all must work on our own and together to make the world a better place to live. It is our choice and why not chose the best answer. The world is in us because we are given the gift of life from our parents, who also were fortunate enough to have the same gift given to them. Everyone is equal in that respect. In this writers mind the most important things in the world next to survival are love, peace, and happiness. If we all strived for those gifts from when we are young, just imagine what a wonderful life we would all have together. We cannot start over, however if we all want to survive and prosper, love, peace and happiness can be the answer. What can you do as an individual to make our earth, our home a better place. Please believe me, destruction and anger will only grow if it is not changed and stopped. No one individual can do this alone it must be practiced by everyone.

So in the end, my final thought is a question. Please write me with your perspective and opinion on what you have just read. Also, God willing, I will continue to write material that is geared toward self change always searching for love, peace and happiness. Thank you all. You are truly my brothers and sisters on this earth.

Notes

_____

_____

_____

_____

_____

_____

_____

_____

_____

Suggested reading

Clason, George S. *The Richest Man In Babylon*. Penguin Books, 1955

Buettner, Dan. Blue Zone *Lessons for Living Longer from the People Who've Lived the Longest*. National Geographic Society, 2008

Giudicissi, Michael. *Changing Lives Achieving Your Untapped Potential*. Robert D. Reed Publishers, 2006

Kaufmann, Walter. *Existentialism From Dostoevsky to Sartre*. The New American Library, 1975

Mattera, Joseph R. *The Road to Financial Success*: *Strategies to Build Personal Wealth and Protecting it*. Authorhouse, 2005

Maxwell, John C. *Your Road Map For Success, You Can Get from Here*. Thomas Nelson, 2002

Nair, M. Gopinathan. *Manage your Mind, Manage your Life*. Xlibris, 2013

Nair, M. Gopinathan. *Mental Science 101*. Amma Publishing Corporation,1997

Scheele, Paul R. *Natural Brilliance Overcome any challenge...at will*. Learning Strategies Corporation, 2000

Tracy, Brian. Goals! *How to Get Everything You Want-Faster Than You Ever Thought Possible*. Berrett-Koeler Publishers, Inc., 2003

Winget, Larry. *Shut Up, Stop Whining& Get A Life*. John Wiley & Sons, Inc., 2004

This is the end of this book.

Remember to live everyday as if it was your last and take the qualities of heaven and convert them into your life.

Printed in the United States
By Bookmasters